Mike
We give thanks Phil. 1:3
for you ...
Paul and Deedee Cox

Name _____

Date _____

They asked each other,
"Were not our hearts burning within us
while he talked with us on the road
and opened the Scriptures to us?"
LUKE 24:32

THE SCRIPTURE CODE

...unlocking spiritual wealth

DEEDEE L. CASS

WESTBOW
PRESS
A DIVISION OF THOMAS NELSON

Unless otherwise noted, all Scripture quotations are from the Holy Bible, New International Version (NIV), copyright 1973, 1978, 1984, International Bible Society. All rights reserved. Used by permission.

Scripture quotations marked (ESV) are from The Holy Bible, English Standard Version. Copyright 2000, 2001 by Crossway Bibles, a division of Good News Publishers. Used by permission. All rights reserved.

Scripture quotations marked (MSG) are from The Message. Copyright (c) by Eugene H. Peterson 1993, 1994, 1995, 1996, 2000, 2001, 2002. Used by permission of NavPress Publishing Group.

WestBow Press books may be ordered through booksellers or by contacting:

WestBow Press
A Division of Thomas Nelson
1663 Liberty Drive
Bloomington, IN 47403
www.westbowpress.com
1-(866) 928-1240

ISBN: 978-1-4497-6220-9 (sc)
ISBN: 978-1-4497-6221-6 (e)
ISBN: 978-1-4497-6222-3 (hbk)
Library of Congress Control Number: 2012914519

Printed in the United States of America
WestBow Press rev. date: 09/27/2012

To Paul—my beloved husband and
partner in service to God

The Code is easy to decipher, but hard to discern.
It is only unlocked by the Word of
God hidden in the heart.

CONTENTS

Part I

Unlocking
Spiritual Wealth

So I say to you: Ask and it will be given to you;
seek and you will find;
knock and the door will be opened to you.
Luke 11:9

FOREWORD

My purpose is that they be encouraged in heart and united in love,
so that they may have the full riches of complete understanding,
in order that they may know the mystery of God, namely,
Christ, in whom are hidden all the treasures of wisdom and knowledge.

COLOSSIANS 2: 2–3

Somewhere on the country road between the church parking lot and my home there was a treasure to be found. It was the Bible that I mindlessly placed on the roof of my car while I buckled my children into their seats.

Somewhere in a classroom where I was teaching there was a treasure to be found. It was the entire book of Genesis that detached from the binding of my worn Bible.

Somewhere on scores of letters, notes, and e-mails I have written there are treasures to be found. They are the verses that I recorded in order to encourage the faith of the recipients.

In all these "somewhere" places there is a treasure to be found. It is the truth that God's Word can be found, but it can never be lost. The psalmist says it best in Psalm 119:89: "Your word, O LORD, is eternal; it stands firm in the heavens."

The eternal nature of the Bible is illustrated for me by a Dry Erase board near the side entrance of my home. It is my practice to write on that board a Scripture verse for all who come and go to consider. Early one morning I was erasing one verse to make way for another when a profound thought came to my mind: *You cannot erase God's Word.* The Bible is a treasure that is indelible and

1

unshakable. How good of God to give us access to His holy and powerful Word! How wise are the ones who avail themselves of the treasure of the Scriptures!

At its heart, *The Scripture Code* is a lesson in amassing spiritual wealth. It is my prayer that you partner with me and invest forward for the sake of your eternal relationship with the Author of the Bible. The treasure is God's to give and yours to find. "Finders keepers" is more than a childhood saying.

PREFACE

The grass withers and the flowers fall,
but the word of our God stands forever.
ISAIAH 40:8

In his junior year in college, my son participated in a study abroad program. As a Spanish major, he was fluent in the language before he set foot on Spanish soil for the first time. After several weeks in Spain, he called me with exciting news. "Mom, I woke up thinking in Spanish this morning!"

The Scripture Code is about thinking in the King's language. It is not about proficiency. It is not about recitation. It is not about spiritual knowledge. *The Scripture Code* is about having God's Word so deeply embedded in your mind and heart that your response to life automatically filters through a biblical perspective.

The Scripture Code (*TSC*) is not just reading a book or learning a memorization technique. *TSC* is a plan of action for a 24/7 intimate relationship with the one who is Himself the Word. *TSC* is not a "commit to memory and you're done" method. Rather, *TSC* is the fulcrum for ongoing life discipline that will maximize your mind's ability to memorize and retain Scripture. What could be better?

Make haste to begin. Vow to persist. Prepare to enter a new arena of spiritual growth. By all means, pray for the Holy Spirit's enablement in making the King's language your very own. I pray that, indeed, you do wake up one morning thinking in God's Word, His powerful and precious Word.

THE VAULT

The law from your mouth is more precious to me
than thousands of pieces of silver and gold.
PSALM 119:72

Who among us would not like to have an endless stash
in our own personal vault? Picture it. Do you need
cash? Go to the vault. Do you need supplies? Go to
the vault. Is there something you just cannot do without? Just go
to the vault. The vault is the dream answer to all of our problems.
Or so we tell ourselves.

The truth is that a dream vault is the problem, not the solution.
We consider a full vault to be the end all of our efforts. Bumper
stickers tell the story of our times: "I owe, I owe—it's off to work
I go"; "The one with the most toys wins." The size of our vault has
come to determine our personal worth. An empty vault drives us
to the edge of our limits. A full vault gives us boundless power
and a worry-free life. Or so we tell ourselves.

What would you do if you knew that the only vault you need
for a life of true wealth is already at your fingertips? You can find
it on your bookshelf and on your grandmother's nightstand. It is
available in hotel rooms across the world, on the back of church
pews, and even in a mobile application on your smart phone. The
only vault you need is the Bible. If God's Word is the answer, then
what is the problem? I say it is time for a new bumper sticker.
Spend your last penny on it. Share your discovery with the car in
your rear-view mirror. *My vault is guaranteed ... by God.*

THE COMBINATION

Buy the truth and do not sell it;
get wisdom, discipline and understanding.
PROVERBS 23:23

The right combination gives access to the vault. Without it, though, the cogs remain still and silent. With the combination, the door swings open. The contents are revealed. The goods are at hand. The valued treasures are available to you.

As a prescribed numerical combination unlocks a vault, *The Scripture Code (TSC)* method of memorization unlocks the mind's ability to commit Bible verses and passages to memory. Inherent in *TSC* is the shorter-longer outcome—shorter time to memorize, and longer retention of God's Word. The goal, however, is not met in the filling of the mind with verses. The goal of *TSC* is to inundate the heart with God's love, God's character, and God's will. With a Scripture-filled heart, we can fully live according to God's plan and purpose. Living according to God's plan and purpose is the true wealth of life.

TSC was born out of my own attempts at Scripture memorization. As a young person, I found that Scripture memorization came easily for me. Several of the verses that I learned during those formidable years framed my decisions as a young adult. Over my thirty years of formal study of God's Word, I have had many opportunities to memorize Bible verses. A few of them made it through. A host of them did not. About five years ago, I discovered that the writing of Scripture was an aid to my aging and crowded mind.

One summer, I made it my goal to memorize several chapters of the Bible. In an effort to learn to praise God in a deeper way, I chose to commit to memory Psalms 145 through 150. These six chapters that cap the beautiful poetry of the book of Psalms are laced with the attributes of God. I practiced by writing out the designated chapters word for word. Eventually, writing all the verses became consuming and cumbersome. Soon I discovered that if I really knew the passage, I could write it out quickly using the first letter of every word. It wasn't long before I had pages and pages of letters representing God's Word in my mind. At various times of the day or night, I would recite my Scripture memory work—either out loud or silently. In time, however, my Scripture writing efforts diminished. I began to notice gaps of phrases and words in my ability to recall segments of scripture that once flowed from my fingertips.

In July of 2011, my enthusiasm for Bible memory returned. After prayerfully considering how I would recapture that which I had lost, I received from the Lord a great idea … reverse the process: use the first letters of each word as a prompt to facilitate memorization. It worked. *The Scripture Code* was born. For me it was a discovery of the combination to an eternal vault. It is my privilege to share my discovery with you. May it provide you with a life-changing combination to unlock the wealth of the Bible.

THE STASH

What would *you* do if you had a personal stash of cash? At the time of this writing, the Mega Millions Lottery is at its highest amount ever: over half a billion dollars. Believe me, millions of ticket holders are out there answering this question on this very day.

To memorize Scripture is to immerse yourself in *the things revealed.* Your heart and mind will become a storehouse of the precepts and principles of the Lord our God. There is much about God and heaven that we will never know until we reach our final destination. In the meantime, God reveals, through His Word, His will and purpose for our lives as we journey on our earthly paths.

For this journey, God has given those who trust His Son for their eternal salvation His precious Holy Spirit. Through the presence of Jesus in our life, we have forgiveness of our sins. Through the indwelling of God's Holy Spirit, we have understanding of the truth of God as revealed in the Bible. *The Scripture Code* bridges the eighteen-inch span between our minds and our hearts. Through the Holy Spirit, the Bible truths committed to memory are deposited in the vault of our soul. Therein lies our stash of **treasures.** What will be the outcome of your soul stash?

I strongly encourage you to make a note of the beneficial outcomes of Scripture memory as you discover them. Here are three of mine to get you started.

☞ **Timeless treasure:** The disciples who so faithfully followed Jesus during His time on earth did not have His words written for them in any version, in either black or red ink. The Word of Jesus came to them on sound waves. Matthew, one of the beloved disciples, recorded the words of Jesus as he heard them. "Heaven and earth will pass away, but my words will never pass away" (Matthew 24:35). Jesus spoke these words to His disciples in a familiar place of His instruction. They were part of a private conversation held on the Mount of Olives. The context of this passage reflects Jesus' desire to instruct His disciples about the temporary nature of the things of this world. It is certain that the disciples came to a point in their lives when they wished they had listened more closely to their teacher. I believe it is also certain that you and I will arrive at the same conclusion. Truthfully, I believe we already have arrived at that place. *TSC* is evidence of our agreement on the need to maximize the Word of God in the age in which God has given us earthly life. Memorizing God's Word is a worthy treasure to pursue. The Bible is our familiar place of Jesus' instruction. Our ledger is the place of our private conversation. Let us not be deterred. Let us sit together with Jesus on the Mount of Olives.

☞ **Trustworthy teaching:** The words of the Bible that were expressed just before the account of Jesus' Sermon on the Mount beckon us to sit at Jesus' feet. "Now when he saw the crowds, he went up on a mountainside and sat down. His disciples came to him, and he began to teach them, saying …" (Matthew 5:1–2). Jesus began His teaching by telling the crowd nine ways to be blessed by God. We know this list as the Beatitudes. While it is true that these words of Jesus are recorded in the New Testament of the Bible, the words that Jesus spoke on the mountain that day were not new words. Whether on the mountain, in the garden, beside the sea, or on the cross, the words of Jesus were quoted from Old Testament passages. Jesus' own divine script validates the teaching of the Bible in its entirety. The words of the apostle Paul in 2 Timothy 3:16–17 further underscore the divinity of Scripture: "All Scripture is God-breathed and is useful for teaching, rebuking, correcting and training in righteousness, so that the man of God may be thoroughly equipped for every good work." The Bible is an inexhaustible source of teaching and training in righteousness. Through the verses we memorize, we have access in every life situation to God's thoughts on the subject. The Word of the Lord will come to mind when we need it. Jesus' disciples recognized the importance of prayer in the life of their Master. The Bible records their desire to learn how to pray: "One day Jesus was praying in a certain place. When he finished, one of his disciples said to him, 'Lord, teach us to pray ...'" (Luke 11:1). Long-term use of *TSC* will transform your prayer life. Without your even thinking about it, God will draw verses from the well of your heart to express praise, worship, confession, thanksgiving, and intercession. The Lord Himself will teach you to pray. *TSC* is a constant beckoning to sit at the feet of Jesus and receive His teaching.

☞ **Priceless relationship:** The twenty-third Psalm beautifully frames the relationship between the Shepherd and His sheep. The Shepherd is all-knowing, all-providing, all-protecting, and all-loving. Jesus' words in John 10 deepen our understanding of the Shepherd and His flock. "I am the good shepherd. The good shepherd lays down his life for the sheep ... I am the good shepherd; I know my sheep and my sheep know me—just as the Father knows me and I know the Father—and I lay down my life for the sheep" (verses 11, 14–15). Oh, the joy of having our relationship with our Good Shepherd reinforced through our days and our nights; in our valleys and on our mountaintops; in our joys and our sorrows; in our temptations and our victories; in our weaknesses and in our strengths; in sickness and in health; in want and in plenty.

- "I have loved you with an everlasting love; I have drawn you with loving-kindness." (Jeremiah 31:3).
- "Come to me, all you who are weary and burdened, and I will give you rest." (Matthew 11:28).
- "And my God will meet all your needs according to his glorious riches in Christ Jesus." (Philippians 4:19).
- "...I will fear no evil, for you are with me; your rod and your staff, they comfort me." (Psalm 23:4).
- "Whatever you do, work at it with all your heart, as working for the Lord, not for men, ..." (Colossians 3:23).
- "For nothing is impossible with God." (Luke 1:37).
- "...for I am the LORD, who heals you." (Exodus 15:26).
- "...my cup overflows." (Psalm 23:5).
- "Great is the LORD and most worthy of praise; his greatness no one can fathom." (Psalm 145:3).

Need I say more?

The act of writing these verses refreshes my spirit. I am so grateful for the opportunity to study the Bible. There is rightness about God's Word. God's assurance and grace pour from it. When I open my Bible, I am transported to God's ideal. Bible memorization keeps that ideal within my grasp. It brings a sense of completion to my soul. The words of the prophet Isaiah say it best: "As the rain and the snow come down from heaven, and do not return to it without watering the earth and making it bud and flourish, so that it yields seed for the sower and bread for the eater, so is my word that goes out from my mouth: It will not return to me empty, but will accomplish what I desire and achieve the purpose for which I sent it" (Isaiah 55:10–11). In "stash terms," God's Word has a 100 percent return. Perhaps it is the perfection of God's Word that delights my heart. Certainly, it is the power and enablement from the Word. Within the worn cover and wrinkled pages of the Book on my nightstand, I find strength and hope and peace. I was prompted to commit this Isaiah passage to memory by a sign I once saw along a rural road in another state. I thank the Lord for the person of faith who took the time to stake the words: "Seek the LORD while he may be found; call on him while he is near" (55:6).

I'd like to share two practical applications of scripture memory with you. Many mental health professionals are encouraging the use of word games to inhibit memory loss. Imagine the benefit of memorizing content that delivers God's blessing and enablement to your life. For me personally, the continual and incremental practice of memorizing the words of God's heart and mind has facilitated my study of the Bible. Verses and phrases come to my mind to support the message I am reading at the moment. It is as though I am drawing from a built-in Bible concordance. In the margins of my Bible, I record the Holy Spirit's reminders of God's language that I have committed to memory. *TSC* enhances my humble effort to know God through His Word.

On a certain corner in the local Amish country lives an Amish family I love to observe. I have seen the father frolicking with his children after a hard day's work in the fields and the mother working faithfully in her garden. Every time I go that way, however, I am taken by the corn crib. The corn crib is always being filled, or else it is filled to the brim. Keeping food for the animals in all seasons seems to be the family goal for the farm. Day after day the dad, the husband, the wife, the mother, and the children farm the land and fill the corn crib. They are about the business of stashing food for the animals that are the heart and soul of their livelihood.

Our livelihood is in Almighty God. His nourishment for our hearts and souls is the Word of God. Make the business of thinking in the King's language a priority objective in your life. A verse from my stash just came to mind: "My soul will be satisfied as with the richest of foods" (Psalm 63:5). May it be so both for you and for me.

Laughing All the Way to the Bank!

And the words of the LORD are flawless,
like silver refined in a furnace of clay,
purified seven times.
PSALM 12:6

When I think of the words *laughing all the way to the bank*, I think of my father. Even now, I can see the smile on his face as he described someone who had achieved monetary success, even though their idea seemed to be counterfeit.

In our culture today, Christianity is viewed as an increasingly counterfeit concept. The principles of our faith are mocked and criticized. Society promotes its own view of God. Government is becoming increasingly devoid of Judeo-Christian ideals and principles. The thought of the present rejection of God brings great lament to our souls. And yet, I recall the words of Jeremiah: "Because of the LORD's great love we are not consumed, for his compassions never fail. They are new every morning; great is your faithfulness. I say to myself, 'The LORD is my portion; therefore I will wait for him'" (Lamentations 3:22–24).

In other words, I am laughing all the way to the bank! It is my pleasure and privilege to share with you one of my deposit tickets. (See "*TSC* Deposit Ticket Bible Verses," Appendix B.)

Forgiveness	T i m b o t c, w i p o f m f t f o s. (Matthew 26:28)
Eternal Life	F G s l t w t h g h o a o S, t w b i h s n p b h e l. (John 3:16)
Peace	P I l w y; m p I g y. (John 14:27)
Joy	... y w f m w j i y p, w e p a y r h. (Psalm 16:11)
Righteousness	... F h h c m w g o s a a m i a r o h r, ... (Isaiah 61:10)
Wisdom	T f o t L i t b o k, ... (Proverbs 1:7)
Purpose	T L w f h p f m; ... (Psalm 138:8)
Hope	B i h w h i t G o J, w h i i t L h G, ... (Psalm 146:5)
Assurance	L u h u t t h w p, f h w p i f. (Hebrews 10:23)

The deposit list for the children of God is boundless. God's Word assures us of all that we have in Christ Jesus. I exhort you to *hide God's word in your heart* so that you too can laugh all the way to the bank. May the Lord grant you a hearty, healthy, and resounding laugh ... all the way to the *bank*! Amen and amen.

THE COUNTING ROOM

For where your treasure is, there your heart will be also.

MATTHEW 6:21

It is in the Counting Room where I discover the depth of riches in my vault. What an awesome thing to consider my compounding spiritual wealth. What began as a quest to memorize God's Word has become an ongoing conversation with God. My meeting with the Lord within the pages of my *Scripture Code* ledger has sensitized me to the sound of His voice as never before. I am like Moses, who pitched a tent outside the camp. In that tent Moses conversed face to face with the living God. The story of Moses' God meetings is found in Exodus 33. "Now Moses used to take a tent and pitch it outside the camp some distance away, calling it the 'tent of meeting' ... As Moses went into the tent, the pillar of cloud would come down and stay at the entrance, while the LORD spoke with Moses ... The LORD would speak to Moses face to face, as a man speaks with his friend" (verses 7, 9, 11).

The *pillar of cloud* is with you in the form of God's Holy Spirit. Your *Scripture Code* ledger is your *tent of meeting*. It is a place of ongoing two-way conversation with God. He reveals what He wants you to know for living a life of godliness. You reveal to God the depth of your desire to be His friend. In the *tent of meeting* ...

He speaks His love ... you are loved.

He lights the path … you are sure-footed.

He exposes sin … you are convicted.

He forgives … you are forgiven.

He comforts … you are at peace.

He extends mercy … you are redeemed.

He bestows grace … you are refreshed.

He reveals His power … you are empowered.

He demonstrates His faithfulness … you are faithful.

He appears as Sovereign … you are confident.

He shows His strength … you are strong.

He imparts wisdom … you are discerning.

He reflects His glory … you are transformed.

Come, then, let us pitch our *Scripture Code* tents outside the camp. The wealth of God awaits us. Let us pursue spiritual wealth with all our hearts and minds and strength.

> *May the Lord direct your hearts into God's*
> *love and Christ's perseverance.*
> 2 THESSALONIANS 3:5

AFTERWORD

The Code is easy to decipher, but hard to discern.
It is only unlocked by the Word of God hidden in the heart.

As you invest increasing amounts of time in memorizing Scripture through *The Scripture Code*, the riddle above will make perfect sense. When you look at the verses and passages written in your Scripture Code ledger, you will immediately recognize that *TSC* is merely using the first letters of the words of Scripture as a clue to the entire word … **easy to decipher**. However, if you do not have the Bible words ingrained in your mind and heart, recognition of the words in your ledger will be impossible … **hard to discern**.

The last words of Moses to the Israelites have merit as we embrace the value of *hiding God's word in our heart*. He spoke to them as they were about to enter the promised land. In all of these thousands of years since they were first spoken, these words have not lost their power or their eternal value. They are God-breathed words to you as your faith grows and matures in the promised land of life in Jesus Christ. One more thing: when you wake up thinking in the King's language, praise God! Your life in Christ will never be the same again.

F t w o m i y h a m;
t t a s o y h a b t o y f.
T t t y c,
t a t w y s a h a w y w a t r,
w y l d a w y g u.
(DEUTERONOMY 11:18–19)

The Last Word

*As for man, his days are like grass,
he flourishes like a flower of the field;
the wind blows over it and it is gone,
and its place remembers it no more.*

*But from everlasting to everlasting
the LORD's love is with those who fear him,
and his righteousness with their children's children—
with those who keep his covenant
and remember to obey his precepts.*
PSALM 103:15–18

Part II

Building Spiritual Wealth

Here I am! I stand at the door and knock.
If anyone hears my voice and opens the door,
I will come in and eat with him, and he with me.

Revelation 3:20

THE LEDGER

... I will put my law in their minds and write it on their hearts.
I will be their God, and they will be my people.

JEREMIAH 31:33

Bankers and ledgers go together. There must always be an account of the contents of the vault. Ledgers record transactions. The assets listed in a ledger are only as credible as the actual worth of the commodity stored in the vault.

Your Scripture Code ledger is a blocked journal where you will list your memory verses in *The Scripture Code* notation. Entering specific verses and passages of Scripture will serve to record the voice of God as spoken to you through His Word. It will become a measure of wisdom and understanding that you have gained through incremental and consistent consideration of the Bible. Your ledger will be the avenue to a heart overflowing with the treasure of knowing God. Through your Scripture Code ledger, you will learn to cherish "every word that comes out of the mouth of God" (Matthew 4:4). Your ledger will be your record, teacher, and trusted friend. It will become a place where you have learned to rely heavily on God's Holy Spirit to do a great work in your life. Let us, then, begin our entries in our Scripture Code ledger.

Setting up your ledger

1. At the beginning of the blocked paper section of
    TSC enter Psalm 119:11. (I use pencil in my ledger.)
    Enter it as written in your Bible first. Then enter it
    using the first letter of each word.

    *   *I have hidden your word in my heart that I may not
        sin against you.*
    *   Psalm 19:11 I h h y w i m h t I m n s a y.

    These words will remind you of the ultimate goal of
    the Christian life: to bring glory to God and to please
    God in all that you say and do and think. The psalmist
    expressed it this way in Psalm19:13: "Keep your servant
    also from willful sins; may they not rule over me. Then
    I will be blameless, innocent of great transgression." The
    Word of God is a powerful weapon against *willful sins*.
    Keep your arsenal of the Word stocked and up to date
    in your memory.

2. Choose the translation of the Bible that is familiar
    to you. Because of the general nature of their
    content, paraphrased translations are not best for
    memorizing.

    *   A sampling of Bible Versions that lend themselves
        to *TSC*: New American Standard Version
        (NASV), English Standard Version (ESV), King
        James Version (KJV), New International Version
        (NIV), New King James Version (NKJV).

3. Make a list of familiar and meaningful Bible verses
    and passages. Over the years, I'm certain you have

learned many individual verses, probably more than you think. List your favorite verses. A list on a sticky note inside of your ledger will give you a good start. Check off your list as each one is entered in your ledger. Do not hesitate to memorize whole chapters of the Bible. You will find the literary construction of whole passages an aid to memorization. Themes of the Bible are brilliant and will make perfect sense to you. Memorizing in context facilitates the memory process. The Beatitudes, the Ten Commandments, John 15, Psalm 1, Psalm 19, and Mary's Song (Luke 1:46–50) are musts for your list of passages.

- Give *TSC* a try on this familiar verse of the church.

  John 3:16 KJV   F G s l t w, t h g h o b S, t w b i h s n p, b h e l.

- Take note of the themes of *love* and *friendship* in the following Bible passage. They will be an aid to memorizing by leading you from one verse to another. **John 15:9–15 NIV** (emphasis added): "As the Father has **loved** me, so have I **loved** you. Now remain in my **love**. If you obey my commands, you will remain in my **love**, just as I have obeyed my Father's commands and remain in his **love**. I have told you this so that my joy may be in you and your joy may be complete. My command is this: **Love** each other as I have **loved** you. Greater **love** has no man than this, that he lay down his life for his **friends**. You are my **friends** if you do what I command. I no longer call you servants, because a servant does not know his master's business. Instead, I call you **friends**, for everything I have learned from my Father I have made known to you."

4. For your first SC ledger entry, choose a passage of Scripture. A Psalm is a good place to start. Psalm 23 or Psalm 100 will give you a strong beginning to your memorization via *TSC*. Do not hesitate to use a chapter or passage that you have already committed to memory. Beginning with familiar verses enables you to get right into the deeper aspects of this system of memorizing.

   • Below is a Psalm you may know. Allow the letters to prompt your mind for the next word.
   Psalm 23 ESV
   T L i m s; I s n w.
      H m m l d i g p.
   H l m b s w.
      H r m s.
   H l m i p o r
      f h n s.
   E t I w t t v o t s o d,
      I w f n e,
   f y a w m;
      y r a y s,
      t c m.
   Y p a t b m
      i t p o m e;

y a m h w o;
m c o.
S g a m s f m
a t d o m l,
a I s d i t h o t L
f.

5. As you approach building spiritual wealth by internalizing the Word of God, keep in mind that *TSC* is not a devotional. Nor is it a Bible study. *The Scripture Code* is a discipline that needs to be exercised and developed. Please understand, however, that *TSC* is not intended to replace or usurp your personal time in God's Word. As a matter of fact, the key to *TSC* success is directly related to daily devotions and ongoing Bible study. The more time you spend in the Scriptures, the more apt you are to hear and recognize God's voice. In God's Word you will hear His call to holiness, faithfulness, and service to the King. Your consistent time in the Bible will fuel your desire to *hide God's word in your heart*. Your commitment to memorizing through *The Scripture Code* will produce a harvest of righteousness. "God made him who had no sin to be sin for us, so that in him we might become the righteousness of God" (2 Corinthians 5:21). Now, there is a vault treasure if ever there was one!

6. Enter as you go. Your ledger lines will increase as you master the entries. Always have a new Scripture ready to record. Add it to your sticky note list. You will be

surprised how many times God will impress upon you something He wants to specifically speak into you. Learn to listen for it. Your next work may come in your time of daily devotion, in church, or from a source that surprises you. God is everywhere. Listen for His voice!

Mastering *The Scripture Code*

1. When actually entering your memory selections in *The Scripture Code*, you will need your Bible and your ledger. Begin by writing the first letter of each word of the verse or passage. At first, your eyes will go back and forth from Bible to ledger until all first letters are entered. Use capital letters and punctuation as they are used in your Bible. As you progress, you will discover that this process of transferring the words into your ledger is the first step in your memory process.

2. Arrange your memory selections according to the phrases as they are used in the Bible. Use of indentations and separate lines will become an aid to memorizing. You do not need to include the verse numbers. However, you may want to put a line (_____) after the natural breaks and sections. This will give you a frame of reference which will kindle your ability to *hide God's word in your heart.*

3. Continual practice in this savvy method of Bible memorization will develop your skills. You will become astute in looking for clues—hyphens,

dashes, capital letters, exclamation points. You can set up your own clues. For instance, you may decide to use an ampersand (&) in place of the **a** for the word and. The first letter capitals of Jesus, God, and Lord will prove very helpful. Repeated words and phrases will trigger your recognition. The words *so that* always get my attention in the Bible because they often denote a desired scriptural result. Therefore, I underline **s t** when it stands for *so that*. *Therefore* is a bridge word in the Bible. Using the code **Tf** (in one square of the graphed page) may trigger your recall of a whole section of your ledger. You can also aid memorization by using two letters in one block for compound words. For example, *firstfruits* can be noted as **ff**. This will be one of your most helpful clues.

4. Sometimes, your eyes will drift to the end of a sentence to discern the meaning of a coded word or phrase. In time, the words will flow from your mind, and you will read through your ledger as if the words were complete spellings rather than written in code.

5. If you are just beginning to learn a verse or a passage, do not struggle with words you do not know. Refer to your Bible to refresh your memory. You will know you are well on your way to mastering a section of Scripture when you realize you are not looking it up anymore.

6. After you become familiar with your Code entries, give yourself ample time for recall. Work on the surrounding words. Ask the Lord to remind you. You will be thrilled when you suddenly remember what a few minutes before was a mystery.

7. Dating your ledger entries will make them a marker of a specific time when God spoke to you from His Word.

8. When you begin going through your ledger, point to each letter with your pen or pencil. It will establish a memory cadence. Your mind will learn to prompt you with the next word in time with the cadence of your point. Soon the cadence will disappear, and your pen or pencil will be gliding across your ledger page. Amen to that!

9. Diligence is required as it is with any new effort. "Reading" through your ledger regularly will enhance your ability to memorize. Eventually, you will be able to use it as a book. My practice is to systematically do *TSC* at night before bed. In this way, the words are fresh in my mind when I sleep. More important, the Word has opportunity to bless me during my rest. I urge you to train yourself to immediately begin reciting your memory repertoire in your mind if you are awakened in the night. It serves to quiet your active mind and put you back to sleep. It has been my experience to fall asleep on one verse and wake-up

reciting at the same place. The next day, you can fill in any gaps or parts you could not remember. All this is part of *TSC* memorization process.

10. Take the *TSC* test. Write your memory work in *TSC*. When the words flow from your mind in first letter format, you are well on your way to thinking in the King's language. Writing in *TSC* is also an efficient way to use small blocks of time to fortify your scripture memory efforts.

11. *Scripture Code* with a friend or in a small group. Have fun with it. Begin a Scripture Code club. Your shared commitment and common goal will stimulate your efforts to pursue spiritual wealth through scripture memory. Get together to encourage one another and share how God is using *TSC* to teach and guide you through life. (See "*TSC* Questions for Deeper Thought"—Appendix D.)

12. Perhaps your faith experience has never included reading or studying the Bible. To you I say, "This is the day the LORD has made; let us rejoice and be glad in it" (Psalm 118:24). You have been bankrupt far too long. It is time to rollover your resources into your *TSC* account. Before you is a vault of the infinite riches of God. Begin now to access its contents by recording and memorizing the verses found on the pages of this book. God has already spoken to you through them. He has already called you to know

Him through His Word. Let me share with you a verse that always draws me into the Bible. "Blessed are those who hunger and thirst after righteousness, for they will be filled" (Matthew 5:6). Go ahead. Satisfy your appetite for God, and be glad! (See "*TSC* Spiritual Wealth Bible Verses"—Appendix A.)

13. Through incremental use of *TSC* over an extended period you will become able to read your ledger without hesitation and to recite and write Bible verses and passages at will. Both these accomplishments will serve to strengthen your relationship with the Author of the Bible. It doesn't get any better than that!

The one thing to understand about your *SC* ledger is that it is not an accounting of secular poetry, prose, or worldly knowledge. Hebrews 4:12 tells us that "the word of God is living and active. Sharper than any double-edged sword, it penetrates even to dividing soul and spirit, joints and marrow; it judges the thoughts and attitudes of the heart." Every letter of God's Word has the power and potential to transform, give hope, and demonstrate the love of God for His children. *The Scripture Code* will help you bask in God's character and His supreme love for you. Bask away!

My Scripture
Code Ledger

My heart is stirred by a noble theme
as I recite my verses for the king;
my tongue is the pen of a skillful writer.
PSALM 45:1

From my Ledger to your Ledger ...

And this is my prayer: that your love may abound more and more in knowledge and depth of insight, so that you may be able to discern what is best and may be pure and blameless until the day of Christ, filled with the fruit of righteousness that comes through Jesus Christ—to the glory and praise of God. (Philippians 1:9–11)

> *With utmost admiration for your commitment*
> *to know God through His Word,*
> *DeeDee*

WAIT! Before you turn the page I have something to tell you. Deposits have been made in advance into your Scripture Code Ledger. They are to your eternal benefit. They are yours to keep. They will not be withdrawn.

In the top margins of each of the following ledger pages you will find a sampling of verses from the entire Bible. They are written in *The Scripture Code*. There are sixty-six of them—one from every book. Out of all the written Word of God these verses have been chosen to inspire your own pursuit of spiritual wealth. They are intended to draw you into the love of God, fortify your faith in God, and encourage you to apply the Word of God in your life. It is my earnest prayer that the Lord will lead you in your spiritual investment venture. May your corncrib be full and your coffers overflow. (See "*TSC* Sixty-Six"–Appendix C for complete record of 1/66–66/66)

You are at a faith crossroads. I entreat you to press on in the Lord as one who can say yes to the question: *Do you Scripture Code?* Afford yourself the opportunity to deepen your relationship with your Heavenly Father through *hiding His word in your heart.* You have read what I have written about spiritual wealth. Now *bank* on what God has written. Do so for the sake of this generation and the next.

> *But the seed in the good earth—*
> *these are the good-hearts who seize the Word*
> *and hold on no matter what,*
> *sticking with it until there is a harvest.*
> LUKE 8:15 MSG

Numbers 6:24-26 T L b y a k y; t L m h f
s u y a b g t y; t L t h f t y a g y p.

Joshua I:9 H I n c y? B s a c.
D n b t; d n b d, f t L y G w b w y w y g.

47

Ruth 1.16 W y g I w g. a w y s I w s.
Y p w b m p a y G m G.

2 Samuel 22:31 A f G, h w i p,
t w o t L i f. H i a s f a w t r i h.

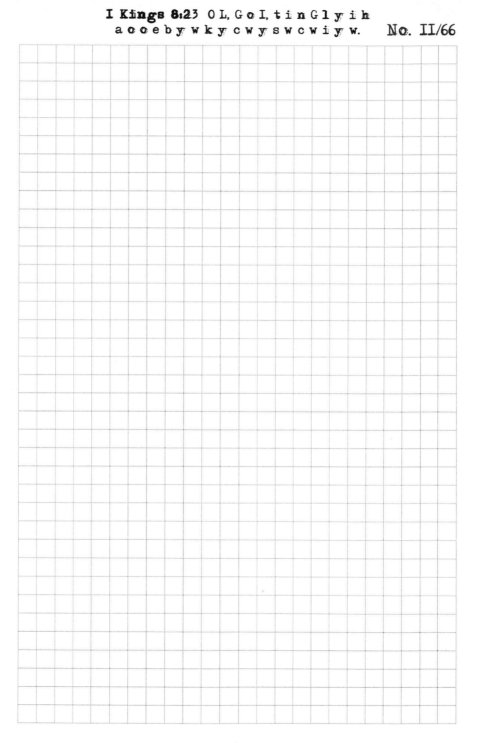

No.12/66   2 Kings 18:6 H h f t t L a d n c t f h;

Nehemiah 9:5

Bbygn.amibeaabap.

No. 18/66   Job 28:28 T f o t L—t i w, a t s e i u.

Proverbs 4:23 A a e, g y h, f i i t w o l.

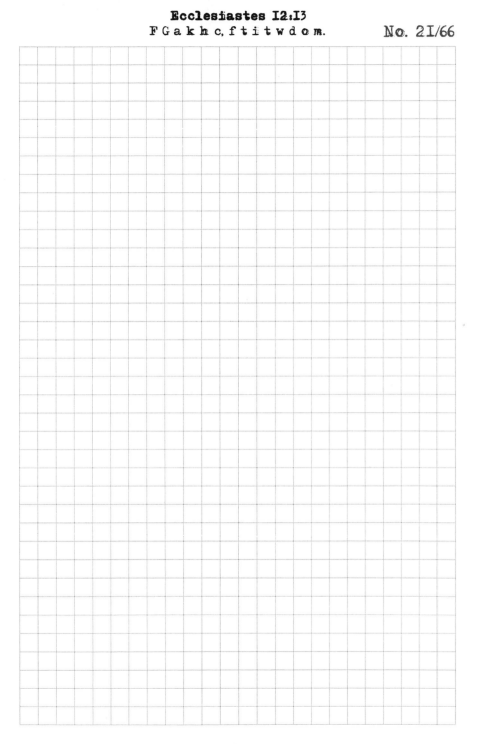

No. 22/66

Song of Songs 2:4

H h t m t t b h, a h b o m i l.

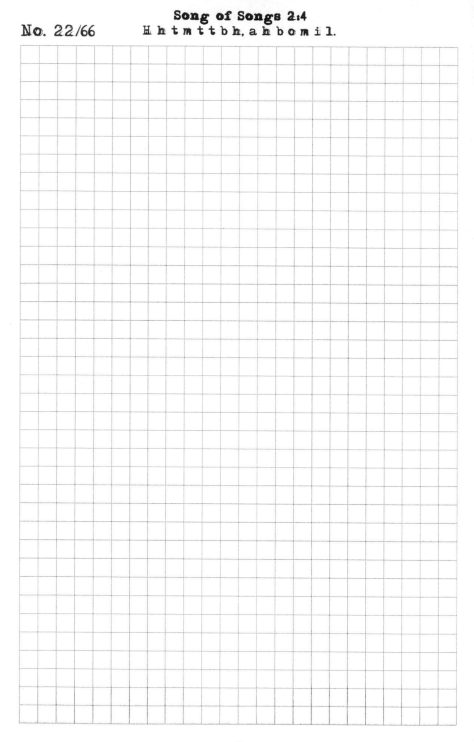

No. 26/66 **Ezekiel 36:26** I w g y a n h a p a n
s i y; I w r f y y h o s a g y a h o f.

By m r t y G, m l a j, a w f y G a.

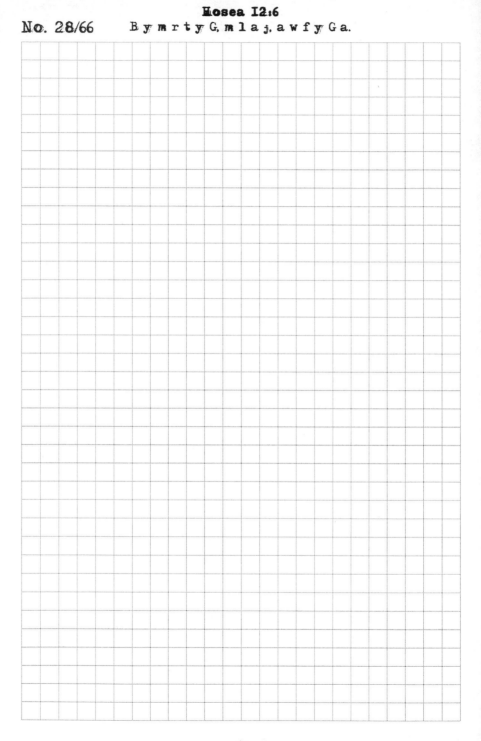

B o M Z w b d; i w b h, a t h o J w p i i.   No. 31/66

Jonah 2:1 I m d I c t t L, a h a m.

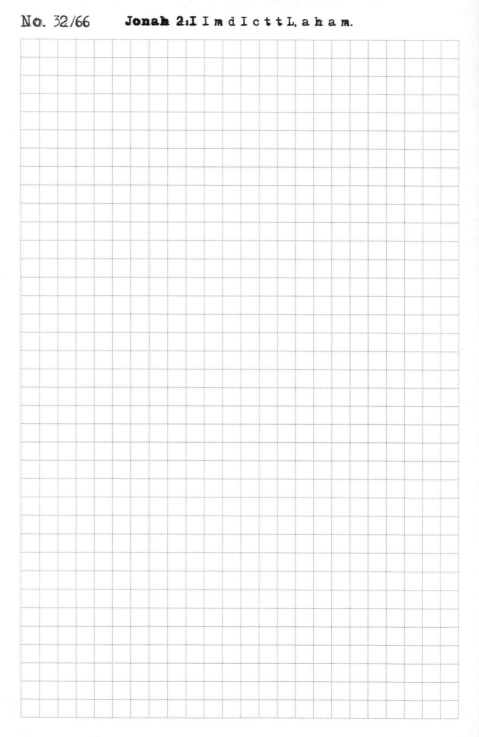

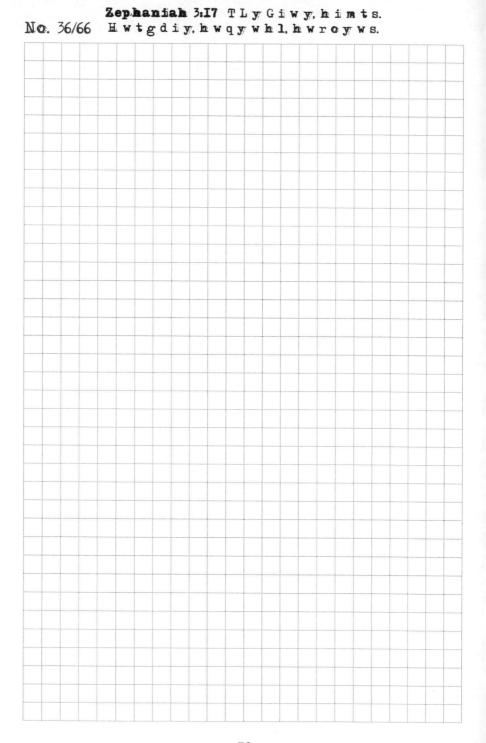

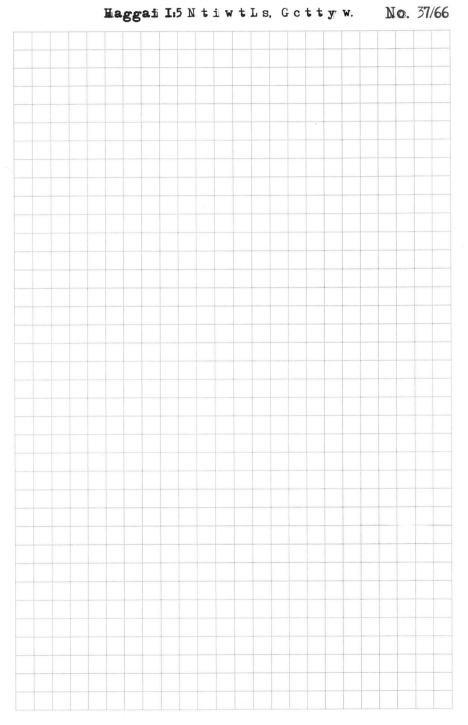

Zechariah 4:6

N b m n b p, b b m S, s t L A.

Matthew 1:21 S w g b t a s, a y a
t g h t n J, b h w s h p f t s.

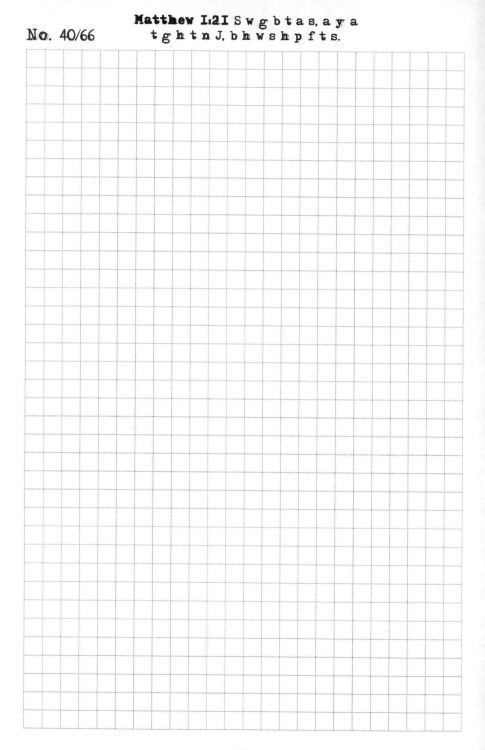

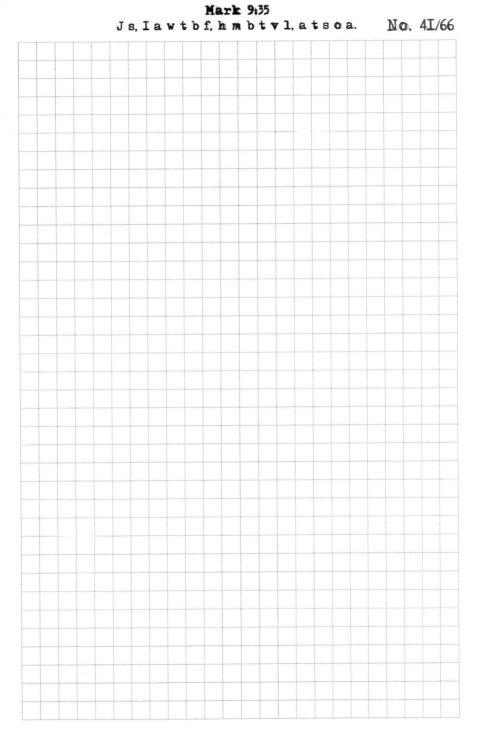

Wgiifamtgtww,aylofhvs?

Acts 20:24 I c m l w n t m . i o I m c
t t t L J h g m t t o t t t g o G g.

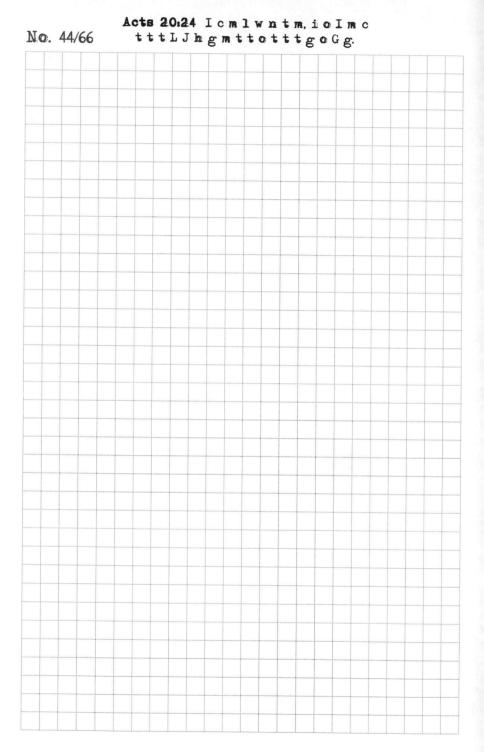

Romans 14:8 I w l, w l t t l, a i w d,
w d t t L. S w w l o d, w b t t L.

No. 45/66

I Corinthians 2:2

F I r t k n w I w w y e J C a h c.

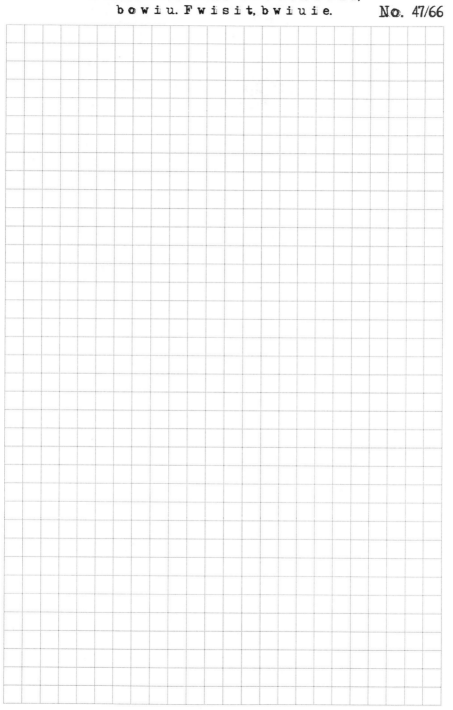

Galatians 6:9 L u n b w i d g.
f a t p t w w r a h i w d n g u.

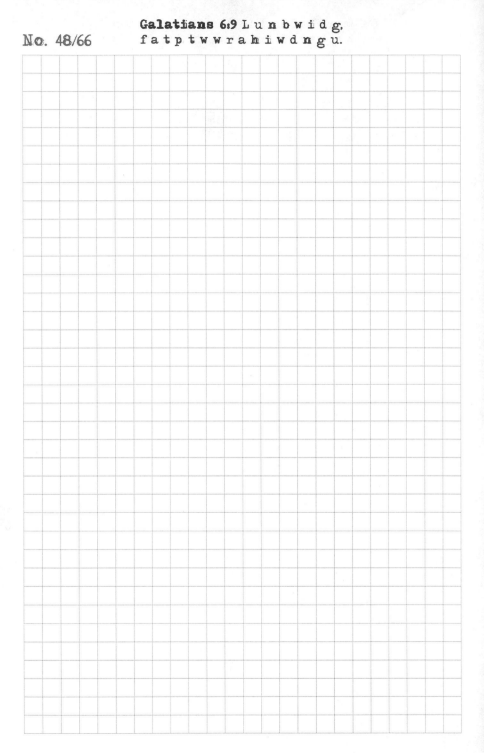

Philippians 4:19

A m G w m a y n a t h g r i C J.

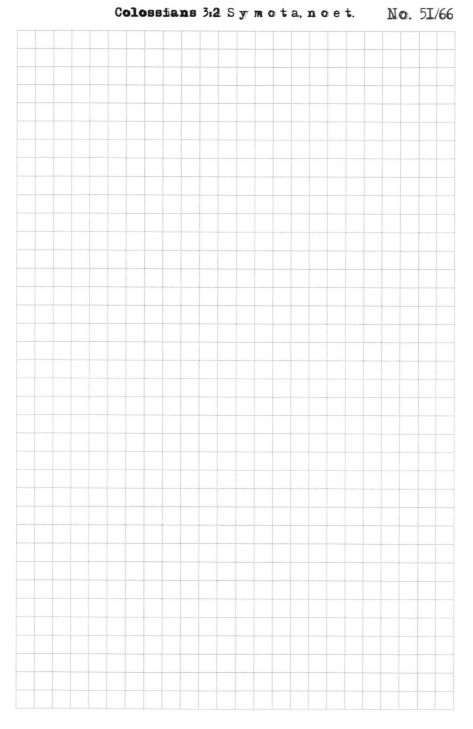

I Thessalonians 5:24
T o w c y i f a h w d i.

2 Thessalonians 3:16 N m t L o p g y
p a a t a i e w. T L b w a o y.

No. 53/66

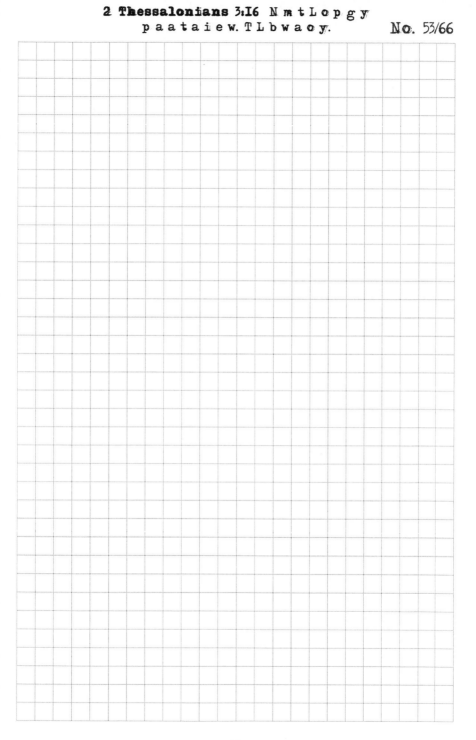

I Timothy 6:18 Itwtwlutftaaf
fftca,sttmthotltitl.

2 Timothy 2:15 D y b t p y t G a o a,
a w w d n n t b a a w c h t w o t.

No. 55/66

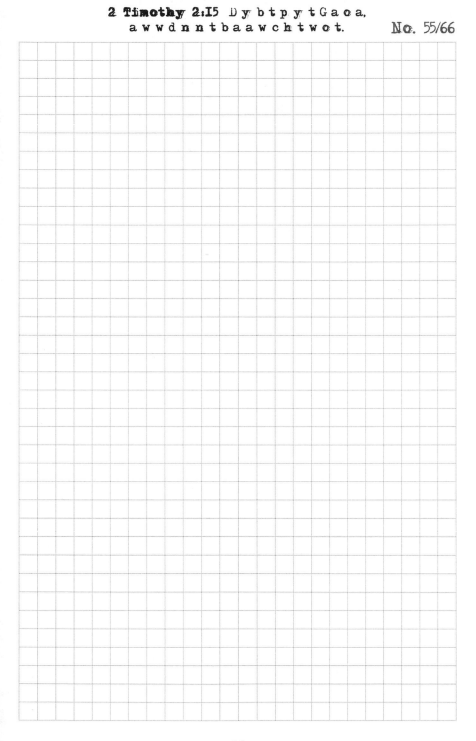

Titus 2:II Ftgo Gtbshatam.

Philemon 6 I p t y m b a i s y f,
s t y w h a f u o e g t w h i C.

No. 57/66

Hebrews 10:23

L u h u t t h w p, f h w p i f.

James 1:5 I a o y l w, h s a G,
w g g t a w f f, a i w b g t h.

No. 59/66

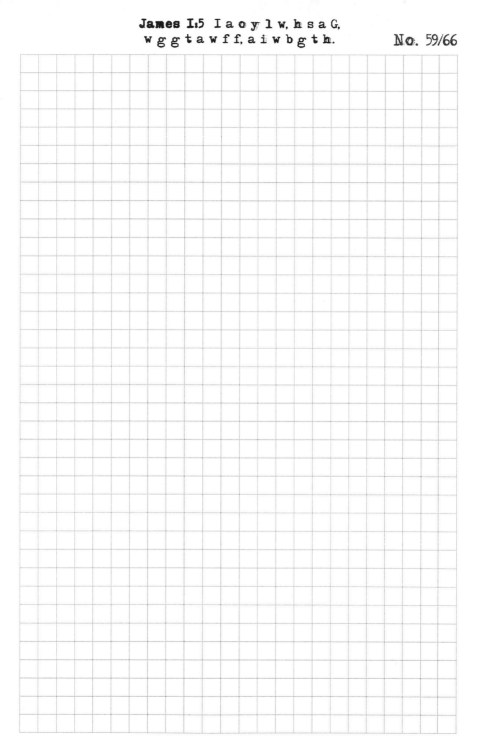

I Peter 3:18

F C d f s o f a, t r f t u, t b y t G.

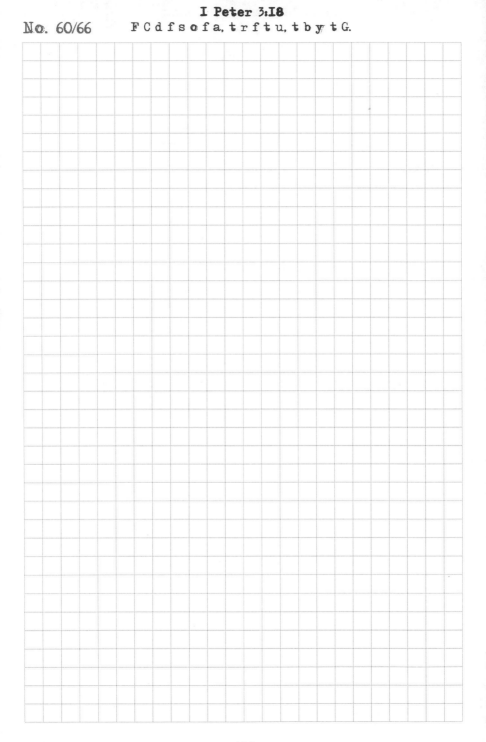

2 Peter 1:3 H d p h g u e w n f l a
g t o k o h w c u b h o g a g.

No. 61/66

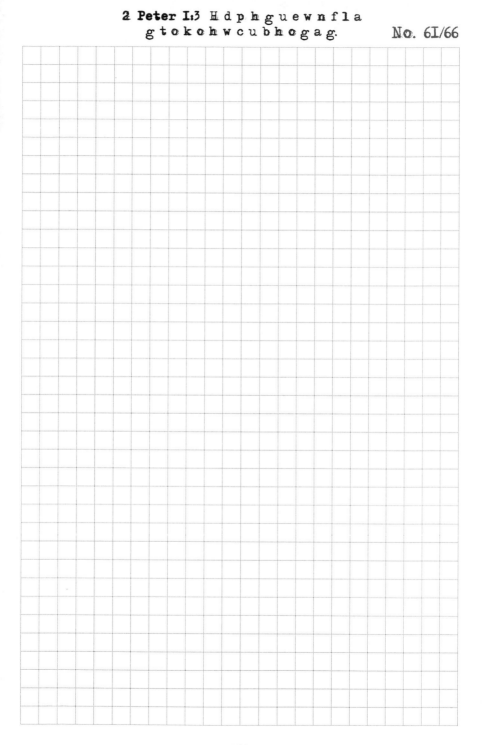

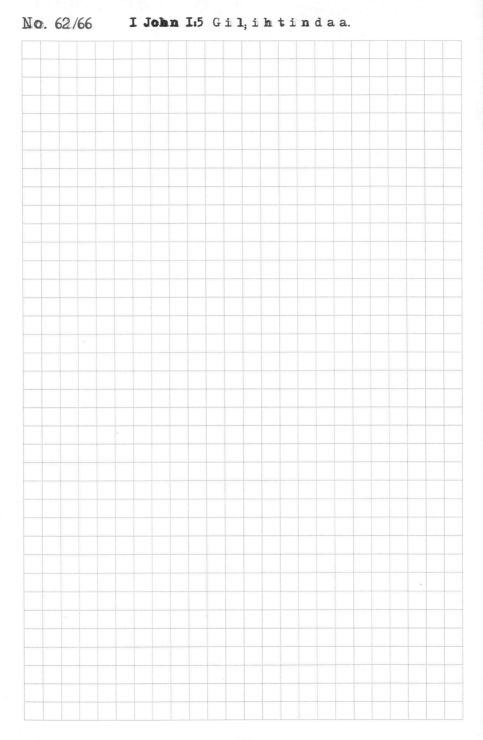

3 **John** 4

No. 64/66   I h n g j t t h t m c a w i t t.

104

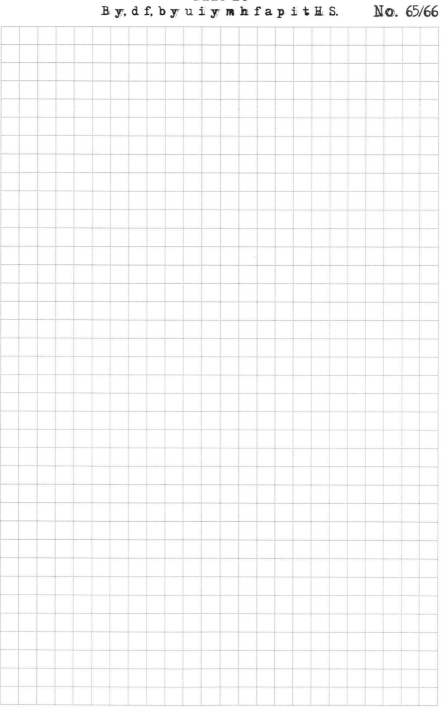

But the man who looks intently into the perfect law that gives freedom,
and continues to do this, not forgetting what he has heard, but doing it—
he will be blessed in what he does.
James 1:25

...c i t g o G. Acts 13:43

Appendix A

TSC Spiritual Wealth Bible Verses

1. "They asked each other, 'Were not our hearts burning within us while he talked with us on the road and opened the Scriptures to us?'" Luke 24:32
2. "So I say to you: Ask and it will be given to you; seek and you will find; knock and the door will be opened to you." Luke 11:9
3. "My purpose is that they be encouraged in heart and united in love, so that they may have the full riches of complete understanding, in order that they may know the mystery of God, namely, Christ, in whom are hidden all the treasures of wisdom and knowledge." Colossians 2: 2–3
4. "The grass withers and the flowers fall, but the word of our God stands forever." Isaiah 40:8
5. "The law from your mouth is more precious to me than thousands of pieces of silver and gold."Psalm 119:72
6. "Buy the truth and do not sell it; get wisdom, discipline and understanding." Proverbs 23:23
7. "The secret things belong to the LORD our God, but the things revealed belong to us and to our children forever, that we may follow all the words of this law." Deuteronomy 29:29

8. "And the words of the LORD are flawless, like silver refined in a furnace of clay, purified seven times." Psalm 12:6

9. "For where your treasure is, there your heart will be also." Matthew 6:21

10. "May the Lord direct your hearts into God's love and Christ's perseverance." 2 Thessalonians 3:5

11. "Fix these words of mine in your hearts and minds; tie them as symbols on your hands and bind them on your foreheads. Teach them to your children, talking about them when you sit at home and when you are walking along the road, when you lie down and when you get up." Deuteronomy 11:18–19

12. "As for man, his days are like grass, he flourishes like a flower of the field; the wind blows over it and it is gone, and its place remembers it no more. But from everlasting to everlasting the LORD's love is with those who fear him, and his righteousness with their children's children—with those who keep his covenant and remember to obey his precepts." Psalm 103:15–18

13. "Here I am! I stand at the door and knock. If anyone hears my voice and opens the door, I will come in and eat with him, and he with me." Revelation 3:20

14. "… I will put my law in their minds and write it on their hearts. I will be their God, and they will be my people." Jeremiah 31:33

15. "My heart is stirred by a noble theme as I recite my verses for the king; my tongue is the pen of a skillful writer." Psalm 45:1

16. "But the seed in the good earth–these are the good-hearts who seize the Word and hold on no matter what, sticking with it until there is a harvest." Luke 8:15 MSG

Appendix B

TSC Deposit Ticket
Bible Verses

Forgiveness "This is my blood of the covenant, which is poured out for many for the forgiveness of sins." Matthew 26:28

Eternal Life "For God so loved the world that he gave his one and only Son, that whoever believes in him shall not perish but have eternal life." John 3:16

Peace "Peace I leave with you; my peace I give you." John 14:27

Joy "…you will fill me with joy in your presence, with eternal pleasures at your right hand." Psalm 16:11

Righteousness "…For he has clothed me with garments of salvation and arrayed me in a robe of righteousness,…" Isaiah 61:10

Wisdom "The fear of the Lord is the beginning of knowledge,…" Proverbs 1:7

Purpose "The LORD will fulfill his purpose for me;…" Psalm 138:8

Hope	"Blessed is he whose help is in the God of Jacob, whose hope is in the LORD his God," Psalm 146:5
Assurance	"Let us hold unswervingly to the hope we profess, for he who promised is faithful." Hebrews 10:23

APPENDIX C

TSC SIXTY–SIX

NO. 1/66–66/66

No. 1/66   **Genesis 1:1** "In the beginning God created the heavens and the earth."

No. 2/66   **Exodus 20:2** "You shall have no other gods before me."

No. 3/66   **Leviticus 18:5** "Keep my decrees and laws, for the man who obeys them will live by them. I am The Lord."

No. 4/66   **Numbers 6:24–26** "The Lord bless you and keep you; the Lord make his face shine upon you and be gracious to you; the Lord turn his face toward you and give you peace."

No. 5/66   **Deuteronomy 3:22** "Do not be afraid of them; the Lord your God himself will fight for you."

No. 6/66   **Joshua 1:9** "Have I not commanded you? Be strong and courageous. Do not be terrified; do not be discouraged, for the Lord your God will be with you wherever you go."

No. 7/66	**Judges 5:3** "I will sing to the LORD, I will sing; I will make music to the LORD, the God of Israel."
No. 8/66	**Ruth 1:16** "Where you go I will go, and where you stay I will stay. Your people will be my people and your God my God."
No. 9/66	**1 Samuel 16:7** "The LORD does not look at the things man looks at. Man looks at the outward appearance, but the LORD looks at the heart."
No. 10/66	**2 Samuel 22:31** "As for God, his way is perfect; the word of the LORD is flawless. He is a shield for all who take refuge in him."
No. 11/66	**1 Kings 8:23** "O LORD, God of Israel, there is no God like you in heaven above or on earth below— you who keep your covenant with your servants who continue wholeheartedly in your way."
No.12/66	**2 Kings 18:6** "He held fast to the Lord and did not cease to follow him;…"
No. 13/66	**1 Chronicles 29:12** "Wealth and honor come from you; you are the ruler of all things."
No.14/66	**2 Chronicles 20:21** "Give thanks to the LORD, for his love endures forever."

No. 15/66   **Ezra 3:11** "He is good; his love to Israel endures forever."

No. 16/66   **Nehemiah 9:5** "Blessed be your glorious name, and may it be exalted above all blessing and praise."

No. 17/66   **Esther 4:14** "And who knows but that you have come to royal position for such a time as this?"

No. 18/66   **Job 28:28** "The fear of the Lord–that is wisdom, and to shun evil is understanding."

No. 19/66   **Psalm 90:12** "Teach us to number our days aright, that we may gain a heart of wisdom."

No. 20/66   **Proverbs 4:23** "Above all else, guard your heart, for it is the wellspring of life."

No. 21/66   **Ecclesiastes 12:13** "Fear God and keep his commandments, for this is the whole duty of man."

No. 22/66   **Song of Songs 2:4** "He has taken me to the banquet hall, and his banner over me is love."

No. 23/66   **Isaiah 26:3** "You will keep in perfect peace him whose mind is steadfast, because he trusts in you."

No. 24/66   **Jeremiah 33:3** "Call to me and I will answer you and tell you great and unsearchable things you do not know."

No. 25/66   **Lamentations 3:22** "Because of the LORD's great love we are not consumed, for his compassions never fail."

No. 26/66   **Ezekiel 36:26** "I will give you a new heart and put a new spirit in you; I will remove from you your heart of stone and give you a heart of flesh."

No. 27/66   **Daniel 2:26** "He reveals deep and hidden things; for he knows what lies in darkness, and light dwells with him."

No. 28/66   **Hosea 12:6** "But you must return to your God; maintain love and justice, and wait for your God always."

No. 29/66   **Joel 2:32** "And everyone who calls on the name of the LORD will be saved;…"

No. 30/66   **Amos 5:24** "But let justice roll on like a river, righteousness like a never–failing stream!"

No. 31/66   **Obadiah 16** "But on Mount Zion will be deliverance; it will be holy, and the house of Jacob will possess its inheritance."

No. 32/66   **Jonah 2:1** "In my distress I called to the LORD, and he answered me."

No. 33/66   **Micah 6:8** "He has shown you, O man, what is good. And what does the LORD require of you? To act justly and to love mercy and to walk humbly with your God."

No. 34/66   **Nahum 1:7** "The LORD is good, a refuge in times of trouble. He cares for those who trust in him,…"

No. 35/66   **Habakkuk 3:19** "The Sovereign LORD is my strength; he makes my feet like the feet of a deer, he enables me to go to the heights."

No. 36/66   **Zephaniah 3:17** "The LORD your God is with you, he is mighty to save. He will take great delight in you, he will quiet you with his love, he will rejoice over you with singing."

No. 37/66   **Haggai 1:5** "Now this is what the LORD says, 'Give careful thought to your ways.'"

No. 38/66   **Zechariah 4:6** "'Not by might nor by power, but by my Spirit,'" says the LORD Almighty.

No. 39/66   **Malachi 3:6** "I the LORD do not change…"

No. 40/66   **Matthew 1:21** "She will give birth to a son, and you are to give him the name Jesus, because he will save his people from their sins."

No. 41/66   **Mark 9:35** " Jesus said, 'If anyone wants to be first, he must be the very last, and the servant of all.'"

No. 42/66   **Luke 9:25** "What good is it for a man to gain the whole world, and yet lose or forfeit his very self?"

No. 43/66   **John 6:27** "Do not work for food that spoils, but for food that endures to eternal life, which the Son of Man will give you."

No. 44/66   **Acts 20:24** "I consider my life worth nothing to me, if only I may complete the task the Lord Jesus has given me—the task of testifying to the gospel of God's grace."

No. 45/66   **Romans 14:8** "If we live, we live to the Lord; and if we die, we die to the Lord. So whether we live or die, we belong to the Lord."

No. 46/66   **1 Corinthians 2:2** "For I resolved to know nothing while I was with you except Jesus Christ and him crucified."

No. 47/66   **2 Corinthians 4:18** "So we fix our eyes not on what is seen, but on what is unseen. For what is seen is temporary, but what is unseen is eternal."

No. 48/66   **Galatians 6:9** "Let us not become weary in doing good, for at the proper time we will reap a harvest if we do not give up."

No. 49/66   **Ephesians 3:12** "In him and through faith in him we may approach God with freedom and confidence."

No. 50/66   **Philippians 4:19** "And my God will meet all your needs according to his glorious riches in Christ Jesus."

No. 51/66   **Colossians 3:2** "Set your minds on things above, not on earthly things."

No. 52/66   **1 Thessalonians 5:24** "The one who calls you is faithful and he will do it."

No. 53/66   **2 Thessalonians 3:16** "Now may the Lord of peace give you peace at all times and in every way. The Lord be with all of you."

No. 54/66   **1 Timothy 6:18** " In this way they will lay up treasures for themselves as a firm foundation for the coming age, so that they may take hold of the life that is truly life."

No. 55/66   **2 Timothy 2:15** "Do your best to present yourself to God as one approved, a workman who does not need to be ashamed and who correctly handles the word of truth."

No. 56/66   **Titus 2:11** "For the grace of God that brings salvation has appeared to all men."

No. 57/66   **Philemon 6** "I pray that you may be active in sharing your faith, so that you will have a full understanding of every good thing we have in Christ."

No.58/66   **Hebrews 10:23** " Let us hold unswervingly to the hope we profess, for he who promised is faithful."

No. 59/66   **James 1:5** "If any of you lacks wisdom, he should ask God, who gives generously to all without finding fault, and it will be given to him."

No. 60/66   **1 Peter 3:18** "For Christ died for sins once for all, the righteous for the unrighteous, to bring you to God."

No. 61/66   **2 Peter 1:3** "His divine power has given us everything we need for life and godliness through our knowledge of him who called us by his own glory and goodness."

No. 62/66   **1 John 1:5** "God is light; in him there is no darkness at all."

No. 63/66   **2 John 6** "And this is love: that we walk in obedience to his commands."

No. 64/66   **3 John 4** "I have no greater joy than to hear that my children are walking in the truth."

No. 65/66 **Jude 20** "But you, dear friends, build yourselves up in your most holy faith and pray in the Holy Spirit."

No. 66/66 **Revelation 22:20** "'Yes, I am coming soon.' Amen. Come, Lord Jesus."

Appendix D

TSC Questions for Deeper Thought

Foreword
1. What do you think is meant by the statement, "God's Word can be found, but it can never be lost"?
2. How would you describe spiritual wealth?

Preface
1. Would you presently describe yourself as one who thinks in "the King's language"?
2. What part does personal discipline play in memorizing scripture?

The Vault
1. What would you do if you discovered an untapped vault of money and valuables?
2. What are some indications that the contents of your vault rule your life?
3. On a scale of 1-10 how familiar are you with the contents of the Bible?
4. Do you personally see increasing your knowledge and understanding of God's Word as valuable?
5. In relation to spiritual wealth, what would your bumper sticker say?

6. What would you do if you knew that the only vault you need for a life of true wealth is already at your fingertips?

The Combination

1. What are some numbers from your past that you remember? (phone numbers, locker combinations etc.)
2. Name some number and letter combinations that are in your memory bank today?
3. Fill in the blank. When asked to memorize scripture, most people of faith say, " I _____ memorize? (can't) Based on your answers to questions one and two, is that really true?
4. Write or share a Bible memory verse that you have memorized.
5. How do you think scripture memory would help you live according to God's plan and purpose?

The Stash

1. How would having a *stash of cash* give you security?
2. Name some things we do not know about God and Heaven?
3. List some truths you do know about God and His Kingdom?
4. How can what we know in our minds differ from what is stored in our hearts?
5. Describe the temporary nature of the things of this world.

6. What does **Matthew 24:35** reveal about God's Word?
7. What value does Jesus place on Old Testament Scripture?
8. What does **2 Timothy 3:16** teach you about the contents of the Bible?
9. Are you ever lacking in your ability to express your thoughts to God in prayer? Explain.
10. Which of the verses in the **Priceless relationship** section are most meaningful to you at this time in your life?
11. Read **Isaiah 55:10-11**. How do Isaiah's words help you to understand the power and value of God's Word?
12. How does scripture memorization help to strengthen the mind?

Laughing All the Way to the Bank!
1. Think about ways that our culture has devalued Christianity?
2. Read each of the recorded **Deposit Ticket Bible Verses** listed in **Appendix B.** Which one would you place at the top of your Bible memorization list?
3. How can people of faith who know God through the Bible make a difference in their families and communities?

The Counting Room
1. Do you believe that God speaks through the Bible?

2. Read aloud the list of ways God reveals Himself to his people. Which of them speak to you?
3. Read **Matthew 6:21**. Think about the relationship between your treasure and your heart. How can you increase your spiritual wealth?

The Ledger

1. Have you ever considered memorizing an entire chapter of the Bible?
2. Do you read your Bible regularly?
3. Have you ever participated in a Bible study?
4. Do you believe that God is personally involved in your daily life? Are you able to give an example of a time when God *spoke* to you through His Word, a person, or circumstance of your life?
5. Name ways in which the Bible is different from secular literature?
6. Are you willing to make a commitment to pursuing spiritual wealth through the memorization of God's Word?

Additional suggestions for maximizing *The Scripture Code*

1. Carefully consider **Appendix A** which lists *The Scripture Code* **Spiritual Wealth Bible Verses**. Ask God to give you understanding of each one. Choose one or two of them to memorize. Enter them into your Scripture Code ledger.
2. Read through *TSC* **Sixty–Six (Appendix C)**. Make note of the Bible verses that are especially meaningful

to you. Find them in your ledger (top margin of each page) and commit them to memory.

3. Share your memory work and your progress with a *Scripture Code* partner. Practice reading your ledger entries out loud to each other.

4. Read God's Word daily and take special note of verses and passages that He impresses on your heart. Add them to your ledger.

5. Read a chapter or book of the Bible. Look for themes that would facilitate memorization. Have at it!

ABOUT THE AUTHOR

DeeDee's lifelong practice of Scripture memory has been cultivated through sixteen years as a Community Bible Study Teaching Director. She is committed to instilling in others desire for the pursuit of spiritual wealth through emersion in God's Word. DeeDee and her husband, Paul, live in West Chester, PA. They have a married daughter and son and five grandchildren. It is their privilege to serve in their home as caregivers to their parents.

*'Love the Lord your God with all your heart
and with all your soul and with all your mind
and with all your strength.'*
Mark 12:30 NIV

L t L y G w a y h a w a y s a w a y m a w a y s. Mark 12:30